About the Author

Juliet Constance Eaton was born in Derbyshire on August 1st, 1934. She married in 1958, where she raised three daughters. Juliet taught piano for many years and began writing poetry at a young age, where her faith in God became most present in her later writings. For this book, I have selected several poems that reflect her faith and capture her love of nature, through the beautiful imagery that weaves its way through each one. My hope is that all who read them will be inspired and encouraged within the daily grind, just as my beloved mum was.

Seasonal Poems of Serenity

Caroline P. Eaton

Seasonal Poems of Serenity

Olympia Publishers
London

www.olympiapublishers.com
OLYMPIA PAPERBACK EDITION

Copyright © Caroline P Eaton 2023

The right of Caroline P Eaton to be identified as author of this work has been asserted in accordance with sections 77 and 78 of the Copyright, Designs and Patents Act 1988.

All Rights Reserved

No reproduction, copy or transmission of this publication may be made without written permission. No paragraph of this publication may be reproduced, copied or transmitted save with the written permission of the publisher, or in accordance with the provisions of the Copyright Act 1956 (as amended).

Any person who commits any unauthorised act in relation to this publication may be liable to criminal prosecution and civil claims for damage.

A CIP catalogue record for this title is available from the British Library.

ISBN: 978-1-80439-199-0

This is a work of fiction.
Names, characters, places and incidents originate from the writer's imagination. Any resemblance to actual persons, living or dead, is purely coincidental.

First Published in 2023

Olympia Publishers
Tallis House
2 Tallis Street
London
EC4Y 0AB

Printed in Great Britain

Dedication

I dedicate this book to my wonderful mum, who brought joy to all who knew her.

In loving memory of Juliet Constance Eaton, 1st August 1934 – 14th January 2021

This book is a selection of beautiful and reflective poems written by Juliet Constance Eaton.

It is dedicated to her memory, where her poetic words live on to bring hope and joy, even in trying days.

A selection of vibrant poems reflecting on the wonder of creation and seasonal changes both in nature and in life.

In times of such uncertainty, there is an even greater need to focus on the beauty within our world that's often sitting right on our doorsteps but so often missed.

My hope is that Juliet's poems will awaken the simplest of joys, to bring comfort, healing, hope and peace to all who read them.

January

A Snowy Night

Hurry, hurry through the flurry
Of the snowflakes soft and white,
Drifting, shifting o'er the landscape
As the moon forsakes the night.

Transcendental, oh so gentle
As they brush against one's cheek,
Dancing lightly, they have rightly
Made the air too cold to speak.

Hurry, hurry through the flurry
For the flakes are falling fast,
Nearly there now, don't despair now
We are almost home at last.

In the morning, when light's dawning
We shall see the glorious sight,
But the night-time's not the right time
To rejoice with great delight.

I was seeming to be dreaming
That the snow had thawed away,
But on waking, so breathtaking
For each flake was here to stay.

Juliet C Eaton

February

Changes

Yesterday dawned dull and cold
Yet silent lay the breeze,
And silent too the roosting rooks
There huddled in the trees.

No whisper of the things to come
No hint of subtle change,
That may or may not choose a time
All things to rearrange.

The atmosphere seemed thin and still
As earth now held her breath,
And footsteps scurried through the mist
As though escaping death.

Then one by one and two by two
Then three by three and more,
They fell as angels from up high
Through sky's now open door.

At visions dancing on the air
And branches clothed in white,
I gazed upon the changing world
In awe and sheer delight.

A carpet formed beneath my feet
From swirling, feathery flakes,
The laughter pealed from children's lips
For this is what it takes.

To make a winter wish come true
As long before the spring,
The heart can re-awake with joy
And make the valleys ring.

Juliet C Eaton

Live this day

Live this day for what it brings you
It is yours alone to see,
Through the eyes of God's great wisdom
Everything that's meant to be.

It may bring you joy and laughter
Opportunities to shine,
Seize them as a personal blessing
Saying these are His and mine.

God may also in His wisdom
Send a time of pain and trial,
Searching through your inner being
For the strength to cope awhile.

This indeed is only natural
It is not His thoughtless whim,
For His love shall never falter
And He trusts you'll lean on Him.

Never think life should be simple
This is why we turn to God,
Or you'll climb those lonely mountains
With the pain of feet unshod.

Juliet C Eaton

Never in a Million Years

Never in a million years
Would Jesus turn away
A person who was shedding tears
With life in disarray
Never in a million years
Would Jesus ever say
Do not bring your cares and fears
I cannot help today.

Juliet C Eaton

Winter Joys

Their pure white petals trimmed with green
Like ballerinas dance,
And bloom in chilly winter winds
Our gardens to enhance.

The snowdrop's beauty never fails
To thrill those who behold,
The shimmering sight of tiny bells
As each head shall unfold.

The winter Jasmine also flowers
Throughout these long cold days,
And spreads her golden glory
As the sun would shed its rays.

The first shoots of the daffodils
Can usually be seen,
Pushing bravely through the earth
Where one day she'll be queen.

An early primrose shyly peeps
From underneath some ferns,
It isn't springtime yet, of course
But this is what she yearns.

The winter days shall quickly pass
And flowers will bloom once more,
Abundantly in many hues
As freely as before.

Juliet C Eaton

Thoughtful Silence

Through the silence of my thoughts
Oh Lord you hear my voice,
Calling from that distant land
You sought my soul by choice.

A land wherein all hope and peace
Shall weary heart now claim,
And none shall need to shade their eyes
Against a life of shame.

Oh, hear me when I call your name
In whispers soft and low,
For there beneath this joyful smile
My heartache will not go.

For very many times I sinned
A fact I tried to hide,
But swiftly you forgive, oh Lord
And are so slow to chide.

I wish I could forgive myself
It's what you'd have me do,
So I will place my hand in yours
And cling steadfast to you.

Juliet C Eaton

March

Her Shadow Fades

A shadow of her former self
The winter bid goodbye,
As clouds of grey were whisked away
Revealing blue on high.

The days of chill were with us still
Though lesser by degree,
And as the sun stole gently through
The change was clear to see.

A thrush was perched upon a bough
He felt the changes too,
And opened wide his tuneful beak
To serenade the blue.

There followed there a happy theme
As blackbird, even wren,
Popped out to sing a merry note
And popped back in again.

A hint of green had joined the scene
Where blossom soon would thrive,
And one could tell, that all was well
And glad to be alive.

A cloud appeared across the sun
And sprinkled down to earth,
A shower of glistening silver drops
Ensuring fresh new birth.

As if by magic, tiny shoots
Came bursting into sight,
It would appear, this time of year
Was absolutely right.

Juliet C Eaton

April

The quickening throb of nature's heart
Uplifting springtime's voice,
To call upon the slumbering earth
Awake, Arise, Rejoice!

The sun rekindled soothing warmth
And beamed from pastel sky,
Rejuvenating songbird's throat
To sing from branch on high.

The dormant shoots soon sprang to life
And trees were splashed with green,
As April hailed the daffodils
To sway upon the scene.

Catkins graced the woodland dell
Now days were much less cold,
And tiny star like celandines
Revealed their heads of gold.

Clover sprang in meadows sweet
Where streams flowed cool and free,
For through the throb of nature's heart
Spring's joy was ours to see.

Juliet C Eaton

Creation

There came to us a perfect day
Wherein the rays of sun,
Did penetrate the darkest hour
Since life had ere begun.

There stirred beneath that beam of warmth
When moistened by the rain,
All plant life's answer to the plea
Of planet earth's refrain.

Upon each flower, upon each leaf
The drops of crystal dew,
Foretold the future plans of God
To bless the world anew.

The very heart and soul of earth
Responded to the call,
And life in every shape or form
Revered Him one and all.

As eye beheld the miracle
To watch the buds unfold,
Insects filled the sun-drenched air
The story could be told.

Of how creation sprang to life
In God's almighty hand,
And through eternal years of grace
Still hears the Lord's command.

Oh, let us share this wealth of love
And beauty all our days,
For we are here at God's request
To lift our hearts in praise.

Juliet C Eaton

Heart's delight

Picture this delightful scene
Where joy and laughter thrive,
Descending on the morning mist
As April days arrive.

Picture where the snowdrop bloomed
As crocus takes her place,
And pastel primrose greets the world
With soft enchanting face.

While crouching neath the sheltered hedge
Sweet violet hides her smile,
As warbling thrush takes up his stance
Where he will bide awhile.

The music of a rippling stream
Now echoes through the dell,
As diving vole and waterfowl
Have joyous tales to tell.

A willow hangs o'er water's edge
Where kingcups thrive en masse,
And tiny blue forget-me-nots
Now star the fringe of grass.

The blackbird too is overjoyed
In concert with the thrush,
For he will build his secret nest
Within the blackthorn bush.

Let not that early morning shower
Be cause of quiet protest,
For every drop is April's gift
And surely she knows best.

Juliet C Eaton

The Dawning

Let the glory of the dawn
Refresh your waking eyes,
And joyous be the listening ear
As birdsongs drift and rise.

Oh, let the thankful heart reach out
To touch the blooming flower,
Now scenting every inward breath
Upon this breaking hour.

Oh, hearken to the throbbing beat
Of nature's bursting joy,
As birds now hasten to their tasks
For which spring will employ.

The hedge shall boast her fair wild rose
Where bluebell must compete,
And campion filled with poise and charm
Thrives at the wanderers' feet.

Oh, let the glory of the dawn
Greet morning with a smile,
And tell the world with breathless awe
To stop and gaze awhile.

Juliet C Eaton

Maytime

See the streams of sparkling sunlight
Spilling from a pastel sky,
Shimmering like a million diamonds
As the springtime hours slip by.

Morning dawned with sacred promise
Up as early with the lark,
Apple blossom fresh and fragranced
Added zest to sunlight's spark.

Hearken now while waking blackbird
Serenades the new born day,
Pausing only as the robin
Also has his tuneful say.

Take a deep and loving intake
Of a breath so filled with scent,
Where the beauty of the bluebell
Bares her heart with pure intent.

Frail and fragile bloom the roses
Gracing hedge in field and lane,
Cosseted by warmth of sun
But smelling sweeter after rain.

Tiptoe lightly over meadows
Early buttercup now thrives,
There to mingle with the clover
As the warmth of May arrives.

Joy on joy as nature's laughter
So infectious casts its spell,
Breathing word for word that story
Springtime ever loves to tell.

Walk alone or share her passion
As this season is but brief,
For the merry month of Maytime
Is indeed beyond belief.

Juliet C Eaton

Did I See Him?

Did I see Him in the distance
Gazing far, far out to sea?
Dreaming of that other lifetime
Where His thoughts must often be.

Did I see Him 'neath the willow
There beside the rippling stream?
Where again His heart seemed focused
Maybe on a long-lost dream.

I may almost say for certain
There within the bluebell wood,
I could sense His very person
Overwhelming where I stood.

For my soul glowed with emotion
As I breathed the fragrant air,
And the glory of that moment
Told me He was truly there.

Oh, what happiness I treasure
As I view the daily scene,
Splendid in its regal beauty
Where the hills rise lush and green.

Take my hand and wander with me
As this woodland wends its way,
Joining in that joyful knowledge
Jesus lives and shares our day.

Juliet C Eaton

A Summer's Morn

The early morn breaks clear and bright
How short the darkness of the night.
Soon after five the sun will rise
With golden haze across the skies.

And now the joyous blackbird wakes
For him, a summer truly makes.
And dewdrops sparkle on the lawn
Evaporating after dawn.

The virgin air smells fresh and sweet
And daisies throng around the feet.
The rose pervades upon the breeze
A perfume that will ever please.

This sanctity of perfect peace
A summer's morning does release.
These precious moments we may share
And feel God's presence everywhere.

Juliet C Eaton

June

Eventide

Watch as evening shades are stealing
Pink and gold across the sky,
Treasured are these precious moments
Sharing beauty with the eye.

Flight on flight of geese a winging
O'er the face of sinking sun,
Where their cry is ever ringing
Rest your toil for day is done.

Thus the sky now bends to ochre
Dappled on the fading blue,
Where the moon shall peep and sparkle
With the fall of evening dew.

Listen intently for the crickets
As descending on the night,
Distant call of owls in concert
Warms the soul with pure delight.

Bats in search of falling darkness
Swoop upon the cool, clean air,
Filling sights and sounds of evening
With a joy our hearts to share.

Juliet C Eaton

Nightfall

Come the soft and peaceful evening
Crimson glory streaks the sky,
Brushed by gold and silver highlights
Glowing where the wild geese fly.

Hear their cry across the skyline
Plaintive on the evening air,
Flying as in strict formation
Through the sunset, who knows where?

Hear the distant cry of curlew
O'er the reeds by water's rim,
As the sun sinks from our vision
Wild hens take their evening swim.

Come the soft and peaceful twilight
Scent pervades on whispering breeze,
Much enhanced by musk and roses
As the darkness falls with ease.

Moonlight glints upon the water
Where reflected once, the sun,
Pale and golden shines her splendour
Welcome proof that day is done.

Juliet C Eaton

The Journey

Let me grasp upon this moment
Just before I take that leap,
Never more must I look backwards
If I am my faith to keep.

Many times I dreamed and wondered
What the future held for me,
But beyond the great horizon
I was not allowed to see.

Now my soul so light and carefree
Longs to try its new-found wings,
As upon the brink I hover
Where my heart in freedom sings.

I can see those living waters
Washing o'er the gentle shore,
And the sky's eternal sunrise
Gleaming through an open door.

Oh, my heart, it beats like thunder
I must take that winged flight,
For the hand that beckons onwards
Knows and understands my plight.

I have grasped and held that moment
Now my soul must rise with ease,
Way above that earthly orbit
Where the past dissolves and flees.

No, I cannot share my wisdom
No, I cannot soon return,
You must bide with faith and patience
To receive that joy you yearn.

Juliet C Eaton

Step Aside

Step aside and let the future
Overtake the past,
Dwelling not upon the sadness
Fading now at last.

Set at nought the angry moments
And those stinging tears,
We should never carry burdens
Born of yesteryear.

Re-awaken with the sunrise
Greet a bright new day,
Step into a different era
Casting pain away.

Look around and see the blossoms
Gaze upon the sky,
Ask this question of the springtime
"Should my heart still cry?"

"No, oh no," will be the answer,
"Face the world with pride,
I am here to make quite certain
All your tears are dried."

Step aside and greet the future
Pain is all but gone,
Forge ahead in joy and wisdom
You and spring are one.

Juliet C Eaton

He Is Surely There

Through rose's gift of fragrant charm
So too, the lily fair,
I hold no doubt within my heart
That God is truly there.

And where soft breezes kiss the leaves
As blossoms grace the bough,
'Tis He alone whose hands reach forth
To fulfil nature's vow.

For summer speaks through God's own voice
With accents clear and sweet,
And blest by endless song of lark
His message seems complete.

But God still has much more to give
Beneath the sun's warm rays,
Where butterflies and humming bees
Enhance those halcyon days.

And then as evening slowly falls
Suffused with silver light,
The trust and warmth of His great love
Hangs softly on the night.

Yes, through the rose's fragrant charm
And mystic beauty rare,
No doubt could steal into my heart
That God is everywhere.

Juliet C Eaton

July

Thoughts of Summer

The beauty of the dragonfly,
Beneath a crystal sun drenched sky,
And breeze's gently whispered sigh,
As summer time arrives.

The mating birds are filled with joy,
And trust that nothing will destroy,
Their nesting skills which all employ,
Where fledgling safely thrives.

So busy now the bumble bee,
A pleasure both to hear and see,
For nature made her own decree,
They'd strive from dawn till dark.

From flowers abounding everywhere,
Their perfume fills the soft warm air,
And way up high without a care,
There sings the joyful lark.

A pleasure always to one's eyes,
Are brightly coloured butterflies,
And fleecy clouds in pastel skies,
We cannot help but gaze.

Then in the calm of eventide,
The creatures of the dark are spied,
When bats and night moths dip and glide,
To end the long warm days.

But days may sometimes prove too warm,
And humid clouds begin to form,
Resulting in a thunderstorm,
To drench the long-parched ground.

Yet when the sun returns again,
All plant life prospers after rain,
Refreshing earth and swelling grain,
God's hand is quite profound.

Juliet C Eaton

August

The Woodland Path

The winding path wove through the trees
I knew not where it led,
But felt compelled to follow it
With steady, silent tread.

The fallen leaves beneath my feet
Felt springy as I stepped,
And now completely over me
A sense of peace had crept.

A rabbit scampered just ahead
And disappeared from view,
Then further on within the woods
I spied a squirrel or two.

With canopy of leaves above
And trees surrounding me,
It seemed no other world outside
Could ever really be.

At length I rested on a log
Which lay upon the ground,
And from the branches high above
I heard the sweetest sound.

Of thrush and blackbird, chaffinch too
In harmony of voice,
Their carefree song and love of life
Fair made my heart rejoice.

I dared not venture further then
The hour was late that day,
And so retraced the path once more
Lest I should lose my way.

But often now I wander there
For quiet and solitude,
And in this woodland paradise
Find peace of mind renewed.

Juliet C Eaton

Sunrise

Upon the magic of this morn
I gaze in sweet content,
For as the sun attains its height
This hour feels heaven-sent.

A song thrush pours out heart and soul
And skyward, drifts away,
To join angelic hosts above
Whence came this perfect day.

The rose reveals her finest blooms
With fragrance truly rare,
Enhanced by lavender and musk
To grace the morning air.

A silver dew adorns the grass
Where early morning mist,
Before departing with the sun
So silently had kissed.

A skylark soars across the blue
To sing while in mid-flight,
With heartfelt praise, for summer days
Which puts the world to right.

Juliet C Eaton

The View

The picture from my window
Simply took my breath away,
Where mountain peaks caressed the sky
Beneath the sun's bright ray.

The lake shone blue and silver
In the early morning light,
And fir trees graced the mountain slopes
A splendid awesome sight.

A waterfall splashed into view
Cascading through the trees,
While butterflies adorned the flowers
Where too were honey bees.

And from a distance came the sound
Of cattle in the glade,
Where they could graze in quiet content
Then seek the noontide shade.

The canopy of blue and white
Which formed the pastel sky,
Foretold a future warm and bright
A promise from on high.

I gazed upon this magic scene
And breathed the pure clean air,
This moment captured here in time
Was way beyond compare.

Yes, way beyond my wildest dreams
And all my heartfelt hopes,
That one day I would ever tread
Upon these mountain slopes.

Juliet C Eaton

The Buttercup

Oh, dainty yellow buttercup
Enchantress of the scene,
You claim the eye of passers-by
In meadows soft and green.

Your glossy petals search the sky
For precious summer rays,
Such sweet appeal, is oh so real
Enchanting summer days.

Your golden glow may please the eye
As far as one can see,
For when we pass, through luscious grass
That's surely where you'll be.

The summer breeze caresses you
And whispers through your stems,
"That lovely flower, is like a shower
Of priceless golden gems."

Juliet C Eaton

Only a Rose

Oh Rose, oh sweet eternal rose
Let not your flower soon fade,
You grace the earth in summertime
And glow through autumn shade.

Enhancing every playful breeze
With perfume fine and rare,
To gladden all who bide awhile
And take the morning air.

No honey bee or butterfly
Your beauty can resist,
But rest within your tender heart
Where sunrays gently kissed.

Oh Rose, oh sweet, eternal rose
Such splendour you impart,
For you were sent by God alone
To please the human heart.

Juliet C Eaton

September

In Season

Come September, come the autumn
See the multi-coloured leaves,
Drifting from the twigs and branches
What a spell the autumn weaves.

Come September and the harvest
Ever fruitful year by year,
Plums and apples, pears now ripen
Blackberries on the briar appear.

Come the toadstools, brown and shiny
Forming rings around the trees,
Come the mushrooms grazing meadows
Where the spores float on the breeze.

Come October, noontide sunshine
Dries and shrivels when they fall,
But come the autumn winds and raindrops
There will be no leaves at all.

Come the winter cold and sneaking
After autumn's fruitful hand,
Now the scene is bleak and empty
Far across the barren land.

Come the frosts and heavy snowfalls
Nature takes her enforced rest,
Come the spring and leaves awaken
But await the earth's request.

To unfold her blooms of beauty
White and purple, pink and gold,
Let the spring now tell her story
One worth telling must be told.

Come the seasons each in order
Bringing forth a wealth of change,
As the summer follows springtime
Scenes again will rearrange.

Warmth and sunshine hales the morning
Comes the plant life's rapid growth,
Trees are clothed in leafy wonder
This is summer's sacred oath.

But the autumn soon will follow
Foggy dawn, then sun and rain,
Falling leaves and ripening produce
As the cycle starts again.

Juliet C Eaton

October

Autumn

The summer time has quickly passed
We see no more her face,
In fond remembrance all will fade
As autumn takes her place.

Before us stretch the country lanes
The trees now almost bare,
As fallen leaves of rust and brown
Are scattered everywhere.

This season is the time for rain
This cannot be denied,
For brooks and rivers overflow
And flood the countryside.

At last when skies of grey are clear
The weather's once more fine,
We tread the carpet neath our feet
Of sweetly smelling pine.

Where blossom grew upon the hedge
Now berries hang instead,
Providing food for hungry birds
When ripened into red.

Around the trees in fields and woods
The mushrooms shyly peep,
While dormice cheerfully search for food
Preparing soon to sleep.

Those flowers which once looked bright and fair
Have withered more each day,
But now the fruits are soft and ripe
To help us on our way.

And juicy blackberries large and sweet
Are laden to the ground,
With gifts of fruit for winter store
The autumn doth abound.

Juliet C Eaton

Dappled Is

Dappled is the morning skyline
Drifting o'er the distant hill,
Where the swallow once ascended
Summer's wish to thus fulfil.

Golden now floats autumn glory
Where each bough bereft of gown,
Tells her own intriguing story
As in leaves, the day shall drown.

Beauty lies arrayed and scattered
Old and russet neath our feet,
Sharing now this time so fruitful
Gathered fully ripe and sweet.

Hedgerows weighted by their berries
Edging lane and fertile field,
Mushrooms peep around the elm trees
Endless is the autumn's yield.

Dappled still the paling skyline
Ebbing soon with sunbeam's life,
Yet the beauty of earth's harvest
Says it all, for joy is rife.

Juliet C Eaton

Perplexing Times

The power of words, the might of song
The closeness of a touch,
That sense of all awareness
When a glance means oh so much.

The moment when a silent move
Like a hesitating hand,
Appears to reach across the gulf
To say I understand.

These little things are life's great gifts
Which frequently impart,
The joy of love or sympathy
To soothe an aching heart.

Stand not alone in times of stress
For someone will be there,
With gentle smile and listening ear
Perplexing times to share.

Juliet C Eaton

November

Squirrel Talk

Little squirrel, little squirrel
On this frosty morn,
You are searching for your breakfast
Please don't look forlorn.

I can find a bag of goodies
Nuts and sunflower seeds,
These I keep for hungry bluetits
But they'll serve your needs.

Underneath my ancient fruit trees
Lie some apple cores,
I can see that you have noticed
Take them, they are yours.

Little squirrel swiftly climbing
Up my damson tree,
When you reach the topmost branches
Tell me what you see.

You may catch a glimpse of heaven
Way above the sky,
But I'm sure you'll keep your secret
Till the day you die.

Little squirrel, please remember
Never feel despair,
When you're sad, or cold and hungry
I am always there.

Juliet C Eaton

Softly, Slowly

Softly, slowly daylight's waning
Joining hands with evening mist,
Trembling o'er the fragrant meadows
Moistened now where dews have kissed.

Softly, slowly dusk is falling
Coaxing in the coming night,
Where the oak and ash like spectres
Bow before the moon's first light.

Gazing upwards through the branches
As a myriad of stars display,
Could this wonder of the moment
Be recalled by light of day?

Softly, slowly clouds now drifting
O'er the face of silent moon,
Darkness thus seems all prevailing
Daylight cannot come too soon.

But the rainfall sweet and gentle
Is but just a short-lived shower,
Bidding moon again re-scatter
Glory on the midnight hour.

Softly, slowly daylight's fading
Mingling with that moment brief,
When the calm of mystic nightfall
Overshadows pain and grief.

Juliet C Eaton

Silver Trail

Silver, trail the threads of moonlight
Weaving patterns through the frost,
Where the tapestry of winter
O'er the branches lie embossed.

Golden peeps the glow of starlight
Thereupon the meadow hoar,
Where the buttercups and daisy
For the present dance no more.

Silver, trail the threads of moonlight
Carving inroads through the air,
Seeking out those icy fingers
Where no other soul would dare.

Hearken now, the peace is broken
As the winged owl in flight,
Shall proclaim her need of freedom
To descend upon the night.

Earth lies hypnotised in stillness
Where the solid lake and pond,
Shiver 'neath the leafless birches
In the copses way beyond.

Silver, trail the threads of moonlight
From a cold and cloudless sky,
Where the diamond jewels of midnight
Dance in awe on winter's sigh.

For this moment is but priceless
And will hold its beauteous sway,
Till those bitter winds of challenge
Sweep the moon and stars away.

Juliet C Eaton

December

A Christmas Song

The star twinkled brightly from clear skies above,
To tell of the saviour who brought heavenly love.
To Mary and Joseph this message I gave,
"Your Son who is blessed, the whole world shall save."

Said Mary to Joseph, "What can this all be?
He is but an infant, all men can see."
Said Joseph to Mary, "Have faith and be strong,
This star is from God and it cannot be wrong."

Thus Joseph and Mary together they stayed,
To watch o'er the Babe and to Heaven they prayed.
That God in His wisdom would teach them their worth,
For guiding the child who is King of the earth.

Juliet C Eaton

Christmas Joy

When Christmas time is drawing near
And rain turns into sleet,
We hear the sound of children
Singing carols in the street.

The trees are draped with tinsel
And aglow with twinkling lights,
Most kitchens smell of baking
And a mixture of delights.

The schools are giving concerts
And the fun of Christmas fairs,
They re-enact the birth of Christ
With carols, plays and prayers.

The children go to super-stores
At night-time in the town,
To visit dear old Santa Claus
With beard and scarlet gown.

He promises them lovely gifts
And lots of food and fun,
And after they have talked to him
Their Christmas has begun.

The scene is almost perfect
If the snow should choose to fall,
It makes the Christmas cards seem real
And fun is had by all.

But this may not bring happiness
And we should stop to think,
Of those who suffer hopelessness
With little food or drink.

Perhaps they're old and lonely
Or are victims of a war,
Oh yes! I hear you now reply
We've heard it all before.

But when you share your festive joy
Upon this Christmas day,
Remember those less fortunate
And quietly kneel and pray.

Juliet C Eaton

On this last page, there is one final poem that Juliet wrote especially for the day of her funeral, which is both moving and comforting.
A true gem within the treasure trove of her beautiful poetry.

Warm and Free

Should this day be wreathed in sunshine
Glowing from a sky of blue,
Should the day be showered with raindrops
Nought would alter what I do.

For this day is truly my day
And I cannot now afford,
To allow one single moment
To withhold me from my Lord.

For surely, I have spent a lifetime
With a picture in my mind,
Of that moment He would ask me
To leave all my cares behind.

So, if the day is wreathed in sunlight
Or maybe there's frost or snow,
I will ask the Lord to bless you
As I bid you let me go.

Love, I know surrounds you always
As indeed it did for me,
And I'll trust you'll feel no sadness
For my heart is warm and free.

Juliet C Eaton